The Masks

Claire Gifford

BookLeaf
Publishing

India | USA | UK

The Masks We Wear © 2023 Claire Gifford

Presentation by *BookLeaf Publishing*

Web: www.bookleafpub.com

E-mail: info@bookleafpub.com

ISBN: 9789358318579

First edition 2023

For Cody, Oakley and all my loved ones

ACKNOWLEDGEMENT

Thank you to everyone for reading my first little book and giving me the courage to get writing more.

Thank you especially to my Mum for being my last minute proofreader and critic!

PREFACE

In my second little poetry book I have included a couple of oldies among a new selection of poems written throughout the year and during a twenty-one day writing challenge.

A Blossom Song

A blossom song,
A scent so sweet
It lights up the darkest room.

A spring relief
From winter's thief,
That falls from the tree so soon.

The Crazies

It's the crazies again,
Filling my head.
Creeping inside,
With sorrow and dread.
The pills are not working
As they should tonight.
I'm feeling fuzzy and distanced,
But too tired to fight.
The thumping in my mind,
Drowns out any logical thought.
I try to push it through,
But it only gets caught
Inside a web of fatigue and shame.
I give up
And I have only myself to blame.
I have had enough,
Put the crazies to bed.
Try to sleep
And think of nothing instead.

Dream

Bigger than you and me,
So much wonder to see.
I hope and dream,
And drift away,
Into the space between.

Falling

Are we falling into
Something untrue?
Are we taking this to the edge
Of reality?
In a bid to be free.
Or is this keeping us locked inside?

A Lullaby

Sleep away your sorrows,
Sleep away your fears,
Don't you worry
For I am here.

Sleep in hope,
And sleep in peace,
Sleep my baby,
Sleep and dream.

Summer Wine

Sipping sweet wine,
In the summer-time.
Soothing melodic songs
In an intensely ravenous heat.
There is a cool breeze in the air
Keeping me from falling asleep.

Feeling ditzy and reminiscent
Of summers gone by.
Memories entice a revisit back
To that free and indulgent high.

Intoxicating drinks flow
With dancing delights!
When days seemed to last,
Way into the night.

How I long again,
For that dreaming wonder.
For those carefree summer-times.

Imagination

The imagination in my child's eye
Is a wonder to behold.
A horse named Lucy - he will ride,
A dragon - he will scold.
Now we are hiding
In a bed cover cave,
There is a frightful monster creeping out there!
He tells me to be brave!
My sweet little boy,
With his superhero cape,
He will save the world
On his imaginary escape!

Fairy Garden

I build a fairy garden
In the flower bed.
Little shells without their host,
With ivy draping overhead.
I pile up little stones,
To make a table and chairs.
They can feast on all the red berries,
That I place there.
Collecting soft roses,
I place the petals in a pile.
A tiny blanket I make for them,
To rest themselves for a little while.

Time

Time passing by,
Fears not of what comes.
Even when we die
Time does not freeze.
Into infinity
Time never ends.
Does time ever mend?

Is there a reason, for what we do?
Have we time
To see this through?
And if not, why do we need
To know the time we do not see
And realise it matters not
What we do and what we do not.
Time is what keeps us sane
Time and time again.

She

She walks with a grace,
Far behind her years,
With a knowing of a great future to be.
She is the envy
Of all her peers,
She is the epitome of being free.

Hello Autumn

Hello autumn,
My long awaited friend!
Come to visit me
Once again!

You bring your chill
And misty air,
Your harsh wind
And golden flare.

On a dry day,
I kick the leaves,
Blood red, mustard yellow
And beautiful burgundy.

Your scene is picture perfect
With the memories you invoke,
From Halloween nights,
To the hot bonfire smoke.

And in the wake of festive cheer,
Winter ends another year.
Good bye to Pumpkin Lattes
And farewell to Mulled wine.

I look forward to your visit next time.

I Am A Witch

I am a witch, they say,
A lonely old hag.
Nestled and scheming away,
They know nothing of me with my herbal bag.

I summon the devil and do his bidding,
My cat is my only friend.
I speak of charms over my cauldron boiling,
I praise the spirits for the good weather they
send.

I am not the witch they think of me.
If only they tried to understand,
A kind soul, they would see.

Urban Legend

The crows and ravens stare
Through the whisper of the trees.
Their haunting glare,
It follows me.

Dogs can sense it's near,
I hear them cry at night!

Fear creeps in,
I remember the tale
A creature tall and thin,
A most heinous fright!

A telephone rings,
Do not answer the call
For you know not where
The curse will fall.

Do not gaze into the black mirror,
For something sinister will see.
Stealing your soul,
And locking it away,
Somewhere between realities!

These urban legends haunt my dreams,

Twisting and replacing folklore.
These stories take hold of our fears,
Yet we long to hear more!

Tales

What tales do these walls tell?
The creaky floors
And long forgotten halls.
Unpolished tables sit bare,
A lonely chair,
Who once sat there?
An empty black fireplace,
Left cold and unused.
Dust covered books stacked unloved,
Up a twisting staircase,
Leading to vacant rooms.
What mysteries dwell behind those doors to uncover?
What trinkets to find,
And tales to discover.

Demons

Can I find
You in my mind?
The Demon that's been draining me.

Can I catch
And throw you out?
Can I ever be truly free?

Will you keep on dragging me down
Deep into your burning pit.
My soul is scorched and now is lost
Somewhere I cannot save it.

The icy caves pull me in,
Is this the Ninth Circle of Hell?
Have I become what I fear the most?
A traitor to myself.

The Masks We Wear

Painted smiles and lit up eyes,
These are the masks we hide behind.
A beauty filter face we use to disguise,
Some existence, we look to find.

Concealing our true self, unaware,
These are the masks we wear.
Convinced this world is better seen,
Undercover behind a screen.

Just Another Day

Another sunrise
Another yawn
Another stretch
Another dawn
Another shiver
Another kiss
Another 'good morning'
Another wish
Another coffee
Another deep breath
Another taste
Another 'are we there yet?'
Another headache
Another moment of calm
Another sunset
Another alarm.

Breaking

There you go again,
Breaking her down.
Closing her in
And watching her drown.

You keep lighting the fumes
Left from the fire,
That you spread through her mind
All for your own desire.

Ghost

Energies remain
As bodies fade,
A ghostly reminder in times past,
Imprinted on the air
As a monochrome photograph.

Buildings absorb
Feelings left behind,
Emotion is a powerful source.
Hatred lingers and madness entwines
With the souls that visit in force.

Never Say Goodbye

Twisting the twilight sky to escape,
Lost in a wilderness of make-believe.
Just to feel
Something willing to be real,
This haunting presence won't leave.

Stuck there like a clouded sky.
Disguising my judgement,
Lost in my cry.

All I write is nonsense,
Unable to describe.
These feelings bring me deeper inside
A vacuum of self-doubt and punishment.
A collapsed star In which I am forced to hide.

One look from you makes me smile,
Longing to be in your gaze.
All outside you is an empty haze.

And I melt away, back into that twilight sky.
Wanting you to never say goodbye.

Festive Scents

Festive scents in the air tonight,
Orange, spice,
And all those delights.
Nutmeg and rum,
Tastes of seasons gone,
Hot coffee and cocoa to keep us warm.
Crackling flames and fire smoke,
Pine needle aroma,
And floral bespoke
Displays of twinkling starry lights.
There is something special in the air tonight!

Milton Keynes UK
Ingram Content Group UK Ltd.
UKHW021102170524
442867UK00014B/741